SUPERPOWERS ACTIVATED

Discovering The Magic

Debbie Donaldson

Cover design by: Jennifer Gonzalez
Copy editing by: Lyn Collier
Printed in the United States of America

In Memory of Doris
This book is dedicated to my mother Doris. She gave
me life and told me I could do anything I set my
mind to. Though she often struggeled with her own
self-confidence, her Superpower was Love.

ACKNOWLEDGEMENTS

Inspiration for this book came from more sources than I have room to mention by name. I would like to thank both the believers and the skeptics in my life. They provided me with a sounding board and fueled my passion for acknowledging the good in all of us.

A special thank you goes to my husband Jamie for his endless love and support.

Thank you to my son Jason, daughter Melanie and step-daughter Julie. They were the first to read the manuscript and provide insight. They didn't know at the time their
Superpowers were an inspiration for many that were chosen for the book.

I will be eternally grateful to:

Lyn Collier who provided copy editing and valuable moral support.
Jennifer Gonzalez who brought the book to life with her inspiring graphic arts talents.
Joshua Szurgot, the photographer who captured my Superpower Happiness.

It is truly liberating to be surrounded by people who have faith, believe in and challenge me at the same time. Through their Superpowers, I continue to learn and discover my own.

I am truly grateful!

Debbie

"Human Superpowers are the many gifts and talents we are born with.

They are also the skills we develop through experiences along our life's journey."

Debbie Donaldson

FROM THE AUTHOR

When I began writing this book in the spring of 2015, I couldn't have imagined the devastating events that would begin unfolding later in the year and how the early stages of this book would help me though.

The idea for a Superpowers book first came to me when I was reading my own daily journal where I occasionally wrote words and their descriptions based on something I had observed or someone who inspired me that day.

One evening as I was looking back on the words and descriptions jotted down over several years. It occurred to me that the words I had written are true human Superpowers. The descriptions I'd written were examples of how these Superpowers were exemplified in the behaviors of my family, friends and colleagues.

When I came across the word Joy in my journal, I remembered the day I had written it down. I was having a difficult day and went to talk it over with my friend at work. She was literally glowing, so I asked her how her day was going. She shared with me a funny video a client had sent her. After we both had a good laugh, she asked me what I came to talk with her about. After lamenting about my situation, she said every day when she leaves for work her partner takes her by the hands and says, "no matter what happens today, never let them steal your Joy." Those words were profound. I told her that her Superpower was Joy and how much her ability to share her Joy made my day better.

That evening when I pulled out my journal and remembered what happened, I realized it was time to capture these words and descriptions into a book and share them with others.

Since I had a full-time job during the week, over the spring and summer months I excitedly wrote every weekend identifying new Superpowers and giving them descriptions. Near the end of summer, it felt like the book was about 75 percent complete. But suddenly, I felt stalled out. It seemed like something was missing.

I shared the book's concept with a few friends and asked their thoughts. The most common answer I heard was that my friends believed I should include my personal experiences. This was coming from people I respect, trust and who know me best. Although I was reluctant at first, their encouragement convinced me to share more of myself, but I still wasn't sure what to share. Since I hadn't finished identifying all the Superpowers I wanted to write about, I decided my personal experiences could wait until at least 52 Superpowers were identified and written.

As the summer months flew by I continued to add new Superpowers to the list. Although the number of Superpowers seems limitless, my goal of writing 52 Superpowers would ensure there would be at least one new Superpower to contemplate each week, making the book a yearlong journal experience.

During this time, I also thought about my own story and how to incorporate it into the book, but every time I'd try to write something it just felt self-serving and arrogant. I've overcome adversity, but hasn't everyone else? Some of you reading this book have activated many Superpowers and faced many more obstacles. I also believed some of the obstacles and barriers that I had to overcome were a result of choices I had made, not circumstances beyond my control.

At this time, I couldn't accept that overcoming self-inflicted obstacles meant I had Superpowers.

Again, I reached out to a supportive friend to talk it over. She asked me a question. "What are your Superpowers?" In that simple question it dawned on me that I had been very comfortable looking at how Superpowers manifested in other people. But, anytime I began thinking about having Superpowers myself, I was uncomfortable and a little self-conscience, even with my own private thoughts. Now someone was asking me to say out loud the thoughts I had been unwilling to entertain inside my own head.

That enlightening conversation helped me begin to get a tiny bit more comfortable acknowledging my own Superpowers without feeling like I was a conceited, boorish braggart. Yes, I was very judgmental about acknowledging my own Superpowers. These feelings also helped me realize there are probably others like me who will have difficulty seeing their own Superpowers and may need help with some prompting questions that will provide real life examples to focus on.

Happiness was the Superpower I immediately recognized in myself during the conversation with my friend. She agreed and pointed out a few others. And as you'll soon learn a little later in my story, I discovered and embraced many more over the following months. In the meantime, I began including some thought-provoking starter sentences for each Superpower. As the sentences are completed, the examples of that Superpower come to life. I also wrote "Discovering the Magic" the chapter explaining how I believe our Superpowers develop.

Then, what happened in the fall of 2015 seemed to put my whole life on hold.

I found a lump in my breast during my monthly self-exam and was eventually diagnosed with breast cancer.

Since my mother and grandmother had died of breast cancer, to say I was terrified was an understatement. I knew I couldn't do this alone. My first pro-active response was calling on all my family and close friends for prayer support. I wasn't sure I had enough Faith to face this monster on my own without them. Fortunately, I was able to recruit a worldwide prayer army and felt truly blessed.

Over the following three months I went through test, after test, after test, after test and met with doctor, after doctor, after doctor, after doctor. Finally, it appeared from all the tests and doctor's evaluations that I had found it at an early stage and the cancer was likely contained in the lump. However, only after surgery would we know for sure.

My job in meeting with all the doctors and undergoing so many tests was to understand my options and make decisions for the best and most effective treatment for me. Talk about needing Superpowers. I always considered myself Intuitive, but my Intuition seemed cloudy, so I relied on science and the advice of my doctors, who fortunately were all advising and supporting the same course of action.

With my strong family history of breast cancer and the pre- cancerous tissue that had previously been found in both breasts, I decided surgery was the best option. And to decrease my chances of ever having breast cancer again I decided to have a bilateral mastectomy.

This decision seemed very radical to my friends and family, but my current doctor was the third doctor over a ten-year span who had recommended such a drastic preventive measure. Each time I previously had lumps, but they turned out to be pre-cancerous or benign.

This time I wasn't going to take any more chances. Based on all my research, the odds of cancer developing again in those pre-cancerous breast tissue areas were extremely high. I activated my Warrior Superpower and began my personal battle to eradicate cancer from my body.

I incorporated both medical and holistic approaches to healing. Relaxation through meditation, essential oils and better nutrition were incorporated into my daily routine. As the days passed by waiting for test results, I couldn't help but remember my own Mother's lost battle to cancer. An aggressive form of breast cancer had already spread to her lungs and bones by the time it was discovered in her body.

It was less than three months from her diagnosis to the day we said our last goodbye. She was only 56 years old. I had already surpassed her lifespan and believed I had many more years to live.

However, I began counting the days from discovering the lump in my own breast. One month passed by as I went through tests and doctor appointments.

Occasionally, my resolve to be fully informed would waver. I even considered the possibility that not knowing may be better than all the tests and the suspense of waiting for results. I considered just pretending it wasn't there and maybe it would go away.

Two months passed with more tests needed based on the results of the previous tests. Doubt would creep in and I would question everything.

Three months passed. Gut wrenching thoughts entered my mind. "What if I don't survive this?" I wondered if I should be saying my last goodbyes to family and friends.

Fortunately, I had a good support network of people around me. Even though they didn't all agree with every decision I'd made, no one tried to persuade me to change direction during my moments of weakness and doubt.

During the month leading up to surgery I couldn't help but question if I had done enough to let the people in my life know how much they meant to me and how loved they were.

Just when I would feel the most insecure about survival, someone would reach out and tell me they knew I would come out of this okay.

I didn't do any last-minute prayer bargaining with God because it seemed he was continually sending messengers telling me I was doing all the right things and I would be healthy with this behind me in no time. People had Faith I would survive. So, I began to trust my own Superpower Faith and believe.

Finally, the day of surgery arrived, and I could relax. It felt like the scene of a science fiction movie as I entered the operating room and saw my doctor who was about to remove the monster trying to kill me.

Surgery was a success. However, the doctors discovered the skin above the lump had breast cancer cells. With that knowledge, once the lump, breast tissue and affected skin along with my two sentinel lymph nodes were all removed and analyzed, my doctors recommended chemotherapy.

This was devastating news to me. I was ready to return to my life and put all this behind me after surgery but was now facing several months of grueling treatments

The doctors had not promised, but I had hoped there wouldn't be a need for chemotherapy after the surgery.

Since we removed all the breast tissue and there was no cancer found in my lymph nodes, I did receive the good news that radiation therapy was not needed.

As I braced myself for chemotherapy I was battling a painful, raging infection that had developed around the expanders implanted during surgery to stretch the scar tissue and make room for breast implants and reconstruction. After nearly a month of antibiotics that weren't working, my doctors and I decided to stop the reconstruction, remove the expanders and heal to prepare for chemotherapy.

Throughout the months of testing, surgery and healing, I often thought about completing this book. As I thought about it, somehow it didn't seem like it was enough to just provide a description of Superpowers. Even though I was not working and had the time to devote to writing, it seemed impossible for me to write about Superpowers when every day I was filled with fear, anxiety and doubt about my recovery, my future and even my survival.

How could I possibly identify and write about Superpowers when I felt vulnerable, weak, indecisive and afraid.

The way I survived those gripping, destructive feelings was to occupy my mind. I watched movies and television shows -- some happy, some sad.

I looked for those that would make me laugh and didn't shy away from shows that brought tears. Both were part of my healing process.

I've always enjoyed Disney animated movies. I hadn't seen the movie "Inside Out" and decided to watch it once I was settled into recovery. The previews made it seem like a light- hearted funny movie, so I settled in to be amused. Boy, was I wrong. There were some funny parts, but the movie unleashed every pent-up emotion within me and I cried during most of the movie. What a wonderful release it created in me.

My daily dose of "Ellen" (the Ellen DeGeneres show) helped me heal and I am more grateful than she and her talented production team could ever know. The people she interviewed, their talents, overcoming life struggles, some even battling cancer and her mantra of being "Kind to One Another" gave me Hope. Her comedy routines and games made me laugh, sometimes I laughed so hard I cried. Both laughing and crying seemed to be a cleansing release giving me moments of Serenity.

I read books, listened to music, meditated and prayed. I leaned heavily on my husband Jamie who was an amazing support and Patient Brave Champion for me.

I found Hope in my family members. We talked, shared funny photos and inspiring music even though they all lived in other cities.

Since my doctors recommended limited exposure to other people's germs through much of the time during chemotherapy treatments, friends stayed in touch with gifts, flowers and nutritious food.

I graciously accepted natural and holistic healing ideas, help and prayer support from family, friends and even strangers. Through the services of the American Cancer Society and the Caring Place I connected with others going through cancer treatments and learned how to care for myself better.

Although I like being in control and being the one that people lean on, I accepted all the support, prayers, love and light anyone had to offer.

Writing about Superpowers at this point in time just didn't seem possible. During my darkest moments though, I read through what I had already written. As I was reading one day, it dawned on me that I needed to be reminded. I needed the affirmation that our Superpowers are always there, they are built in.

We develop our Superpowers over time and through life

experiences. They are always there to draw upon when needed. Mine and the Superpowers of others were getting me through the darkest, most insecure days of my life.

My life changed completely when I learned I had cancer. The decisions were daunting.

It seemed like they were the most difficult choices I had ever made in my life. Every choice came with its own set of life altering risks.

It seems odd now to admit that one of the most difficult decisions was to take my doctor's advice and stay home during chemotherapy treatments. It seemed like I was being asked to cut off who I was. I had already missed a couple months of work; how could I be expected to miss even more.

Other people I knew had worked during chemotherapy, but as I learned throughout the treatment and healing process, everybody is different. So, I reluctantly accepted my doctor's strong advice to focus on my treatment and healing.

Who I was before cancer seemed to be connected to what I did. I was the publisher of a successful business newspaper and website, I was on the board of the Better Business Bureau and Junior Achievement, I was the committee chair of the Las Vegas Rotary Club Foundation annual food drive.

The reason all my professional accomplishments seemed so important to me was that I was successful despite the many obstacles I encountered or chose throughout my life. I was abused as a child, dropped out of high school and became a teenage wife and mom.

At the age of twenty-five I was a single Mother raising two children armed with a GED and loads of determination to provide a good life for my children and myself.

Achieving career success, despite being a high school dropout and teenage mom with all the odds against me, became a great source of pride. However, I always seemed to be afraid of losing the momentum and having it all slip away.

After reading the Superpowers that I had written, it occurred to me that my great source of pride was misplaced. Our true value is not in what we do, but in who we are. We can never lose the knowledge, skills and experiences gained over time. Those Superpowers like Bravery and Courage that were activated when I stood up to my childhood abusers are at my disposal anytime they are needed.

In reading the words I had written, I found they helped me reconnect with my true self. After all, in addition to professional accomplishments, I am a loving daughter, wife, sister, mother, grandmother, aunt, friend and much more by being empowered with many of the Superpowers written about in this book. And I am filled with Gratitude every day.

Finding Hope, Joy, Faith, Tranquility and many other Superpowers in those around me gave me strength to draw upon my own Superpowers and heal.

Eventually returning to work was a blessing, but it didn't hold the same spell on me as it had before. When I found myself lamenting that I didn't have the energy I'd had before for attending early-morning or late-evening business events, I realized that I was complaining that I didn't have the energy to be a workaholic like I was before.

I concluded that denying myself proper nutrition, life balance and rest likely contributed to the weakness in my body that allowed cancer its chance, and I wasn't returning to those risky behaviors.

It turned out that I had plenty of energy for the job I was hired to do and began enjoying the adventure even more. Most important is that I truly appreciated the people around me and reveled in the shared Passion for the work we accomplished together.

As you can tell by reading this, I finally completed my story and published the first Superpowers Activated book. Before finishing though, I realized there is another story that needs telling -- yours.

I'll continue my quest to recognize, identify and activate my own Superpowers. In addition, I'll look for ways to connect with others and help conquer the debilitating dark forces we all face, like fear and despair.

There are hundreds of thousands of people suffering at the hands of oppressors every day. Whether those oppressors are unenlightened people, debilitating afflictions or deadly diseases, every person has within them the Superpowers to begin to change, improve and heal.

My belief is that each person reading this is ready to begin discovering the magic of activating their own Superpowers. Like me, you may find it easier to begin by recognizing Superpowers within others that you respect or admire. Hopefully, you'll soon find it just as easy and even more empowering to recognize your own Superpowers.

Every person you encounter benefits in some way by the Superpowers within you that are activated.

As we walk our own paths continuing to activate our unique Superpowers for good, the journey will not always be easy. However, it is possible to conquer the dark side together.

Disclaimer

The contents of this book are intended to inspire those who read to enjoy and enhance a positive, peaceful, healthy lifestyle. The descriptions and definitions are personal interpretations. If you believe the description doesn't fit your beliefs of the words, simply create an interpretation that is more suitable for you.

I am not a medical doctor and do not recommend specific treatments for any disease or illness.

DISCOVERING
THE MAGIC

Human Superpowers are the many gifts and talents we are born with. They are also the skills we develop through experiences along our life's journey.

Your journey began the moment you came into the world. The events, people and places of your early childhood began shaping your Superpowers as you learned and grew. During your childhood you received valuable challenges and opportunities to foster the Superpowers growing within you.

Although we are born with these Superpowers, it is up to us to activate them. Activation includes recognizing our Superpowers, then using them freely for the benefit of ourselves and others.

During the emotionally volatile years of your adolescence, you began identifying with, formulating opinions about or maybe even idolizing heroes and heroines from movies, television or sports. Your own Superpowers may seem insignificant in comparison to your idol's larger-than-life, real, or imagined attributes.

As you mature you begin to place less emphasis on outside influences and more emphasis on your own ideas and opinions. These are important steps in your journey and do not happen at the same chronological age for everyone.

Each human being is unique in their realization of their own Superpowers. Fortunately, we can activate several Superpowers at the same time. We are not limited in the number of Superpowers we have or the number we activate simultaneously. Through use over time, our Superpowers continue to grow in strength and effectiveness.

Life transitions are often challenging. However, your Superpowers continuously emerge and activate to sustain you on your life's journey. Maturing in adulthood is a continuous evolutionary process of enlightenment. Through transitions in your life, you connect on a more conscious level with your own internal power sources.

The definitions and descriptions are open to interpretation. This book is meant to be used as a meditation and journey guide, empowering you to recognize and unlock the magic of your many Superpowers.

Within this book is a description of 53 Superpowers. There are many more Superpowers within you to be discovered and activated.

In using this book as a guide, it may at first be easier to recognize the Superpowers in others around you. As you read the Superpower definitions, take a moment to reflect on an example of a Superpower that you've seen in a friend, colleague or family member.

This initial exercise is a catalyst for identifying and activating your own Superpowers.

It may feel awkward at first to see in yourself the Superpowers you read about here.

Identifying and acknowledging your Superpowers can become as natural as examining the unique features of your face and eyes in a mirror. For example, when you look into the mirror, you see your face, then more specifically you see your eyes and their color, maybe even flecks of a different color in your irises. You get a little closer, look into one eye and see there is a dark or light-colored ring around that iris. You may notice that your pupil contracts a little in diameter as you get closer to the light.

Now, take a closer look at your Superpowers. Take a moment to glance through the list of Superpowers in the table of contents. Go to a Superpower chapter that has a word you are most drawn to or feel may describe you.

The definitions at the beginning of each Superpower chapter are merely a hint at the word's meaning. The chapters start with partial textbook definitions from Merriam-Webster.com or Dictionary.com and then explore them on a different, higher level. Your answers to the questions and the descriptions that follow each word are interpretations of how each Superpower is manifested in you.

Take a moment to write down a time when you felt this Superpower within you. Jot down how you felt and what action you took as a result of this feeling.

Were there benefits realized from activating your Superpower? You may not know them at this time, but if you do, write them down as well.

The temptation will be to stay focused on others. Recognizing and appreciating the Superpowers in those around you is very important and a very good first step in activating your own Superpowers. However uncomfortable it is to focus on your own Superpowers, it will be worth the effort.

The magic of Superpowers is discovered by experiencing them in the actions of those around us; in recognizing them in our own actions; and in how we believe others perceive them in the way we live.

Consider focusing on one Superpower each week. Look for examples of how it comes to life in those around you and in yourself. Complete the sentences for the Superpower at the beginning of the week and again at the end of the week. This awareness may ignite a new passion within you.

How we choose to activate our Superpowers each day defines us. Although there are many people along the way to influence your journey, it is truly your journey.

The choice is always yours and only you can discover the magic in activating the Superpowers within you for good.

The world awaits!

SUPERPOWER CHAPTERS

In the pages ahead, you'll find an abbreviated interpretation of the dictionary definition of each Superpower. On the following page, you'll see a few thought-provoking questions to help you identify these qualities in yourself and others.

Use the weekly journal pages in the back of the book to record your thoughts and feelings about each Superpower.

The last page in each chapter contains a description of how the Superpower manifests when activated.

Superpowers Activated is where the magic happens and "mere mortals" own the power to improve their lives and the world for good.

CHAPTER 1

BALANCE: Defined

- *the ability to move or remain in position without losing control or falling*

BALANCE: In Action

Complete the following sentences:

- *The most Balanced person I know is…*

- *Examples of how they find Balance are…*

- *I know I am Balanced when…*

- *The three most positive observations my closest friends would make about my Superpower Balance are…*

Superpower **BALANCE**

Your life has a rhythm and your Superpower Balance keeps you synchronized even when the world continually challenges your equilibrium.

When it comes to relationships at work, with family and friends, each feel you are giving them your all.

You instinctively know, however, that time for yourself is the key to activating this Superpower that keeps your life and those around you in Balance.

NOTE TO SELF:

BALANCE

is just one of my many Superpowers

CHAPTER 2

BRAVERY: Defined

- *the quality that allows someone to do something dangerous or frightening*

BRAVERY: In Action

Complete the following sentences:

- *The bravest person I know is...*

- *Examples of their most brave actions are...*

- *The most Brave action I ever took was...*

- *The three most positive observations my closest friends would make about my Superpower Bravery are...*

Superpower BRAVERY

Your Bravery has been activated since the first time you took action on something you were afraid to do but forged ahead anyway. A bonus to your Superpower is that you are also Brave for others. Those who follow you sense that your Bravery is like a shield protecting them from what they fear.

Your Bravery guides you and those around you
past fear and doubt to positive action.

NOTE TO SELF:

BRAVERY

is just one of my many Superpowers

CHAPTER 3

BROTHER: Defined

- *a man who is from the same group or country as you*

BROTHER: In Action

Complete the following sentences:

- *The people in my life whom I consider Brothers are…*

- *The experiences we shared that bonded us as Brothers…*

- *I am most proud of the moments I was a Brother when…*

- *The three most positive observations my closest friends would make about my Superpower Brother are…*

Superpower BROTHER

There are many people who have enjoyed and continue to benefit from connecting with you as a Brother. This innate Superpower is a bond that goes beyond blood or family relations. The Superpower Brother may be activated within you regardless of your gender or age.

This incredible Superpower is like an emotional glue that keeps you connected as a Brother, even when facing the most challenging issues.

Those who call you Brother know they can count on you for the best type of support at the exact time it is most needed.

NOTE TO SELF:

BROTHER

is just one of my many Superpowers

CHAPTER 4

CHAMPION: Defined

- *one that stands up for another's rights or honor*

CHAMPION: In Action

Complete the following sentences:

- *The most inspiring Champion I know is...*

- *The results of their actions were...*

- *I have been a Champion for...*

- *The results of my actions were...*

- *The three most positive observations my closest friends would make about my Superpower Champion are...*

Superpower CHAMPION

As a Champion you live this Superpower every day. The tiny spark that lights your Superpower Champion for a company, person or cause ignites a passion that is contagious. You are never content to be the only Champion. As a Champion you engage all your most developed Superpowers to draw in others and inspire them to be Champions as well.

Those that know you want you in their corner and instinctively know you have their back.

NOTE TO SELF:

CHAMPION

is just one of my many Superpowers

CHAPTER 5

COMPASSION: Defined

- *sympathetic consciousness of others' distress, together with a desire to alleviate it*

COMPASSION: In Action

Complete the following sentences:

- *The most compassionate person I know is…*

- *Their Compassion has inspired me most when…*

- *Compassion comes easy for me when…*

- *The three most positive observations my closest friends would make about my Superpower Compassion are…*

Superpower COMPASSION

Your Superpower Compassion is woven through your life like a fine golden net. Each thread is a symbol and reinforcement of your Superpower as you spend time in service to others. Your Compassion grows as you generously give of your time, talents, financial resources and understanding.

When others connect with you, they willingly become caught in your net and begin to weave their own Superpower net of Compassion.

NOTE TO SELF:

COMPASSION

is just one of my many Superpowers

CHAPTER 6

CONFIDENCE: Defined

- *having or showing assurance and self-reliance*

CONFIDENCE: In Action

Complete the following sentences:

- *The person I know with the most Confidence is...*

- *Their acts of Confidence have affected me most when...*

- *My Confidence shines most when...*

- *The three most positive observations my closest friends would make about my Superpower Confidence are...*

Superpower CONFIDENCE

Your Superpower Confidence solidifies within you, especially when challenged. Your emotional skin becomes an armor of steel in the face of adversity.

Your Confidence is an outwardly visible inner drive that forges ahead inspiring others to follow.

NOTE TO SELF:

CONFIDENCE

is just one of my many Superpowers

CHAPTER 7

COURAGE: Defined

- *mental or moral strength to venture, persevere, and withstand danger, fear, or difficulty*

COURAGE: In Action

Complete the following sentences:

- *The most Courageous person I know is...*

- *Their Courageous actions resulted in...*

- *I feel most Courageous when...*

- *The three most positive observations my closest friends would make about my Superpower Courage are...*

Superpower COURAGE

Your Courage takes many forms and is one of your primary Superpowers. Courage acts as a catalyst in activating many of your other Superpowers. The courageous actions you take every day often go unnoticed, even by you. Your Courage guides you in knowing when to speak up for what matters... sit down for what's right... or walk away for the greater good.

Whether your Courageous action is large or small, you wield this incredible Superpower Courage to affect positive change.

NOTE TO SELF:

COURAGE

is just one of my many Superpowers

CHAPTER 8

DREAMER: Defined

- *one who has ideas or conceives projects regarded as impractical*

DREAMER: In Action

Complete the following sentences:

- *The Dreamers I admire most have accomplished...*

- *My greatest Dreams are...*

- *The three most positive observations my closest friends would make about my Superpower Dreamer are...*

Superpower DREAMER

Your ability to imagine the unachievable is what makes your Superpower Dreamer seem more like fantasy. Although others may balk at your visions, this is the Superpower that gave us penicillin, enabled astronauts to walk on the moon and has helped us eradicate many diseases from the planet. You too improve your universe with your dreams.

Dream big, the world will thank you.

NOTE TO SELF:

DREAMER

is just one of my many Superpowers

CHAPTER 9

FAITH: Defined

- *firm belief in something for which there is no proof*

FAITH: In Action

Complete the following sentences:

- *The most Faith-filled person I know is...*

- *Their Faith has...*

- *My Faith has...*

- *The three most positive observations my closest friends would make about my Superpower Faith are...*

Superpower FAITH

Your heart is the vessel of your Superpower Faith. With every beat, your very being is sustained by your Faith. You believe and instinctively know that there are things that can't be seen or proven but are made real by Faith.

Every action you take for yourself and on behalf of others is guided by your life-sustaining Superpower Faith.

NOTE TO SELF:

FAITH

is just one of my many Superpowers

CHAPTER 10

FATHER: Defined

- *one that originates or institutes*

FATHER: In Action

Complete the following sentences:

- *The most responsible Father I know is...*

- *Their actions made a difference by...*

- *As a Father, the moments I'm most proud of are...*

- *The three most positive observations my closest friends would make about my Superpower Father are...*

Superpower FATHER

This Superpower is activated within you the moment you accept responsibility for someone other than yourself. As a Father you have a balance of masculine and feminine qualities that you are quite comfortable drawing on when the time is right. The Superpower Father may be activated within you regardless of your gender or age.

When activated, as a Father, you become the steward of your charges. Whether they are children, members of a group or employees in a company, your words and actions guide and protect. Through your actions as a Father, you also move those in your care toward the realization of their own Superpowers and independence.

Once activated, this Superpower Father becomes part of who you are, not merely what you do.

NOTE TO SELF:

FATHER

is just one of my many Superpowers

CHAPTER 11

FORGIVENESS: Defined

- *to give up resentment of or claim to revenge*

FORGIVENESS: In Action

Complete the following sentences:

- *The most profound act of Forgiveness I experienced happened when...*

- *I've found ways to Forgive and the result was...*

- *The three most positive observations my closest friends would make about my Superpower Forgiveness are...*

Superpower FORGIVENESS

Your Superpower Forgiveness swaddles you and those around you like a warm blanket on a cold night - thawing even the coldest hearts hardened by resentment. There isn't any transgression too large or too small for you to activate this healing Superpower Forgiveness.

NOTE TO SELF:

FORGIVENESS

is just one of my many Superpowers

CHAPTER 12

GRACE: Defined

-   *unmerited divine assistance given humans for their regeneration or sanctification*

GRACE: In Action

Complete the following sentences:

- *At least one person I know who has the Superpower Grace is:*

- *Moments when I experienced Grace in their presence resulted in:*

- *The gift of Grace has changed my life in the following ways:*

- *The three most positive observations my closest friends would make about my Superpower Grace are:*

Superpower GRACE

You bring your Superpower Grace with you everywhere you go. It's like an illuminating cloud of perpetually renewing diamond dust that sprinkles your gift of Grace on everyone in your presence.

The people in your life genuinely feel your gift of Grace after each encounter with you.

NOTE TO SELF:

GRACE

is just one of my many Superpowers

CHAPTER 13

GRATITUDE: Defined

- *appreciative of benefits received*

GRATITUDE: In Action

Complete the following sentences:

- *The three people I am most Grateful for in my life are...*

- *I am also Grateful for...*

- *The Superpowers I am most Grateful for are...*

- *The three most positive observations my closest friends would make about my Superpower Gratitude are...*

Superpower GRATITUDE

Your Superpower Gratitude shines brightest
when it manifests in the appreciation
you show those around you.

Your Gratitude is almost as powerful as a fairy tale magic
wand. When you express your Gratitude for something
specific, more of it appears in your life. For example,
when you express your Gratitude to your friend for
their support and kindness, you'll notice even more
support and kindness from that friend and others.

Gratitude for the people, things and circumstances in your
life is a Superpower you know can never be overused.

NOTE TO SELF:

GRATITUDE

is just one of my many Superpowers

CHAPTER 14

HAPPINESS: Defined

- *a state of well being and contentment*

HAPPINESS: In Action

Complete the following sentences:

- *The Happiest person I know is...*

- *Their Happiness has...*

- *I am Happiest when...*

- *The three most positive observations my closest friends would make about my Superpower Happiness are...*

Superpower Happiness

Your Superpower Happiness comes in multiple forms and is often felt more deeply than it is observed. It is most easily recognized when combined with your Superpower Joy.

When your Superpower Happiness is activated, it is shared freely. With every contact you make, you initiate a Happiness exchange similar to the way a hummingbird flits from flower to flower collecting and leaving behind a bit of pollen from each flower. Your Happiness accumulates, then deposits just the right amount of goodness and nourishment with each person you encounter, leaving them with a sense of Happiness of their own.

NOTE TO SELF:

HAPPINESS

is just one of my many Superpowers

CHAPTER 15

HEALER: Defined

- *to restore to health*

HEALER: In Action

Complete the following sentences:

- *The person in my life with the Superpower Healer is...*

- *I first recognized the Healer Superpower in them when...*

- *I first knew I had the Superpower Healer when...*

- *The three most positive observations my closest friends would make about my Superpower Healer are...*

Superpower HEALER

When needed, you go beyond the science of medicine and tap into your Healing Superpower. It seems like you have always known just what will make a person feel better. A tender touch, an affectionate glance, a familiar and comforting aroma, taste, sound or just listening are only a few of the ways you engage multiple senses in the healing process.

As a Healer your Superpower is an effective complement to modern medicine and quite a mystery to many.

NOTE TO SELF:

HEALER

is just one of my many Superpowers

CHAPTER 16

HOPE: Defined

- *to desire with expectation of obtainment*

HOPE: in Action

Complete the following sentences:

- *The person who inspires Hope in me is...*

- *Their Hope inspired me to...*

- *Hope has changed my life in the following ways...*

- *The three most positive observations my closest friends would make about my Superpower Hope are...*

Superpower HOPE

Hope is the most misunderstood Superpower in your arsenal because it seems passive. Hope is the catalyst for positive change. Your Hope is the spark that creates a chain reaction by first inspiring positive belief, then positive action. Hope then carries you through your actions to affect positive change. The results of this Superpower seem magical.

Holding onto Hope through adversity brings
the greatest rewards - magical indeed.

NOTE TO SELF:

HOPE

is just one of my many Superpowers

CHAPTER 17

HUMILITY: Defined

- *action reflecting, expressing or offered in a spirit of deference*

HUMILITY: in Action

Complete the following sentences:

- *The person I admire most for their Humility is…*

- *Their Humility became obvious when…*

- *My own Humility has resulted in the following unexpected rewards…*

- *The three most positive observations my closest friends would make about my Superpower Humility are…*

Superpower HUMILITY

Your Superpower Humility is an endearing character
trait that draws others to you as you discover and
develop your many incredible Superpowers. It works
like a thermostat keeping you human and approachable
as you grow to understand the many positive effects
your Superpowers have on those around you.

NOTE TO SELF:

HUMILITY

is just one of my many Superpowers

CHAPTER 18

HUMOR Defined

- *characteristic or habitual disposition*

HUMOR: in Action

Complete the following sentences:

- *The person I know with the best sense of Humor is...*

- *Their disposition affects me by...*

- *My own Humor has served me by...*

- *The three most positive observations my closest friends would make about my Superpower Humor are...*

Superpower HUMOR

Your Superpower Humor serves you well by allowing you to provide levity even during the most serious moments. You are adept at wielding this Superpower to bond your team, family or friends with a timely bit of shared laughter.

You take your Superpower Humor seriously and are vigilant about ensuring it is never used at the expense of others.

Although you may enjoy the Humor of professional comedians, your Superpower Humor goes beyond entertainment and is infused into everyday situations, making even difficult circumstances more bearable.

NOTE TO SELF:

HUMOR

is just one of my many Superpowers

CHAPTER 19

IMAGINATION Defined

- *the act or power of forming a mental image of something not present to the senses or never before wholly perceived in reality*

IMAGINATION: in Action

Complete the following sentences:

- *The most imaginative person I know is...*

- *Their Imagination has...*

- *My imagination has led me to discover...*

- *The three most positive observations my closest friends would make about my Superpower Imagination are...*

Superpower IMAGINATION

Your Imagination is the Superpower that has the
greatest impact on continuous improvement.

It's the fuel generated by your Superpower Dreamer. That
same fuel then engages your Superpower Creativity.

The more specific and detailed your Imagination
the easier it is for others to be inspired by and
moved to support making your ideas reality.

NOTE TO SELF:

IMAGINATION

is just one of my many Superpowers

CHAPTER 20

INTEGRITY Defined

- *firm adherence to a code of especially moral or artistic values*

INTEGRITY: in Action

Complete the following sentences:

- *The people who most helped me develop Integrity are...*

- *The most vivid lessons and examples I learned were...*

- *My Integrity has been tested most when...*

- *The three most positive observations my closest friends would make about my Superpower Integrity are...*

Superpower INTEGRITY

Your Superpower Integrity is at its strongest activation power when you are faced with a choice of paths. A choice between right and wrong or good and bad is simple for you with Integrity as your Superpower. The tougher choices between paths of good versus greater-good raise the level of difficulty in your choice and strengthens your resolve with Integrity as your guide.

Although your choices may not always be the most popular, your Superpower Integrity lights the path for others to see the way.

NOTE TO SELF:

INTEGRITY

is just one of my many Superpowers

CHAPTER 21

INTUITION: Defined

- *quick and ready insight*

INTUITION: in Action

Complete the following sentences:

- *The most Intuitive person I know is...*

- *Examples of their Intuition are...*

- *My Intuition has...*

- *The three most positive observations my closest friends would make about my Superpower Intuition are...*

Superpower INTUITION

Your Superpower Intuition is often referred to as your sixth sense. Others are either drawn to or are wary of your keen sense and knowledge about things you cannot immediately prove to be true.

This Superpower is much like your sense of taste in that no two people experience the same exact intensity or flavor. It's also similar to your taste buds, due to the many receptors within you that are taking in information.

How you interpret and take positive action with the information you gather consciously and unconsciously is what makes Intuition one of your most valuable Superpowers.

NOTE TO SELF:

INTUITION

is just one of my many Superpowers

CHAPTER 22

INVENTOR: Defined

- *to produce something for the first time through the use of imagination or of ingenious thinking and experiment*

INVENTOR: in Action

Complete the following sentences:

- *The most inventive person I know is...*

- *I have invented...*

- *The three most positive observations my closest friends would make about my Superpower Inventor are...*

Superpower INVENTOR

Recognizing a problem, then connecting unrelated items that become the solution is so natural for you that it's difficult for you to believe this is your Superpower.

Many times, the problem you solve isn't even recognized by others until you provide the solution with your latest invention.

NOTE TO SELF:

INVENTOR

is just one of my many Superpowers

CHAPTER 23

JOY: Defined

- the emotion of great delight caused by something exceptionally good or satisfying

JOY: in Action

Complete the following sentences:

- *The most Joy-filled person I know is...*

- *I feel Joy most when...*

- *The three most positive observations my closest friends would make about my Superpower Joy are...*

Superpower JOY

Joy is the radiant aura emitting from your soul like sunshine.

Whether you are aware of or oblivious to this special Superpower, the effect is the same. The light from your Joy can be seen and felt by everyone you encounter. It also lights the spark that inspires others to discover the Superpower Joy within themselves.

NOTE TO SELF:

JOY

is just one of my many Superpowers

CHAPTER 24

KINDNESS: Defined

- *treating people with respect*

KINDNESS: in Action

Complete the following sentences:

- *The most Kind person I know is...*

- *When I am Kind...*

- *The three most positive observations my closest friends would make about my Superpower Kindness are...*

Superpower KINDNESS

When your Superpower Kindness is felt by those around you, they are naturally changed for good.

Your Kindness is like the gift of a cool breeze on a warm day, refreshing everyone in its reach. You are generous with your Kindness, and like the breeze, never judging whether those in your path deserve to experience your gift.

NOTE TO SELF:

KINDESS

is just one of my many Superpowers

CHAPTER 25

LEADER: Defined

- *guiding someone or something along the way*

LEADER: in Action

Complete the following sentences:

- *The best Leader I know is...*

- *As a Leader I have experienced...*

- *The three most positive observations my closest friends would make about my Superpower Leader are...*

Superpower LEADER

As a born Leader, your Superpower is visible in the respect shown by those who follow you. As a leader, you do not rely on position power, it is only through personal power that you develop this incredible gift.

In developing your Leadership skills over time, you Lead by example and mutual respect. Your Leader Superpower inspires those who follow you to engage their own various Superpowers and achieve their very best.

NOTE TO SELF:

LEADER

is just one of my many Superpowers

CHAPTER 26

LOGIC: Defined

-       *interrelation or sequence of facts or events
    when seen as inevitable or predictable*

LOGIC: in Action

Complete the following sentences:

- *The person I know who uses Logic most often is...*

- *I most often use Logic when...*

- *The three most positive observations my closest friends would make about my Superpower Logic are...*

Superpower LOGIC

Your Superpower Logic guides you with the uncanny sense of having a map and detailed directions long before anyone else even knows there is a destination.

Although others may not always understand, with Logic you are able to make critical decisions without being encumbered by emotions that may hinder progress. Your Superpower Intuition is the best compliment to your incredible Superpower Logic.

NOTE TO SELF:

LOGIC

is just one of my many Superpowers

CHAPTER 27

LOVE: Defined

- *unselfish, loyal and benevolent concern for the good of another*

LOVE: in Action

Complete the following sentences:

- *The person or people who have shown me Love are...*

- *When giving freely of my Love I have experienced...*

- *The three most positive observations my closest friends would make about my Superpower Love are...*

Superpower LOVE

Your ability to Love unconditionally is your most powerful Superpower. Although love is commonly reciprocated, your Superpower isn't bound by any expectations. Pouring from you like a warm and gentle rain, your Love is the Superpower that heals even the most tortured souls.

NOTE TO SELF:

LOVE

is just one of my many Superpowers

CHAPTER 28

LOYALTY: Defined

- *unswerving in allegiance*

LOYALTY: in Action

Complete the following sentences:

- *The most Loyal person I know is...*

- *When I am Loyal...*

- *The three most positive observations my closest friends would make about my Superpower Loyalty are...*

Superpower LOYALTY

Your Loyalty is activated by a special connection to a person or cause. Your Loyalty is like a magnet drawing others in support of something greater than yourself.

You instinctively know this support and bond creates a far- reaching chain reaction like the ripple effect of a pebble being tossed in a pond.

You are keenly aware of exactly when and where to activate your Superpower Loyalty.

NOTE TO SELF:

LOYALTY

is just one of my many Superpowers

CHAPTER 29

MAN: Defined

- *the individual who can fulfill or has been chosen to fulfill one's requirements*

MAN: in Action

Complete the following sentences:

- *When I think of the one person I count on the most it's...*

- *When I have been chosen or referred to as "the man for the job" the results were...*

- *The three most positive observations my closest friends would make about my Superpower Man are...*

Superpower MAN

This non-gender specific Superpower allows you
to stand out and take charge or serve in support
of those that count on you.

When you are the Man that others rely on, your
magnetism attracts those who have a desire to develop this
Superpower within themselves creating an ever-widening
circle of proteges that can be counted on in times of need.

NOTE TO SELF:

MAN

is just one of my many Superpowers

CHAPTER 30

MOTHER: Defined

- *someone who is an ultimate example*

MOTHER: in Action

Complete the following sentences:

- *The best Mother I know is...*

- *As a Mother, I am most proud of the moments when...*

- *The three most positive observations my closest friends would make about my Superpower Mother are...*

Superpower MOTHER

This Superpower is activated within you
the moment you accept responsibility for
someone else other than yourself.

As a mother you have a balance of feminine and masculine
qualities that you are quite comfortable drawing on when
the time is right. When activated, as a mother, you become
the steward of your charges. Whether they are children,
members of a group or employees in a company, your words
and actions guide and protect. Through your actions as
a mother, you also move those in your care toward the
realization of their own Superpowers and independence.

Once activated, this is one of the Superpowers that
becomes who you are, not merely what you do.

NOTE TO SELF:

MOTHER

is just one of my many Superpowers

CHAPTER 31

PASSION: Defined

- *intense driving feeling or conviction*

PASSION: in Action

Complete the following sentences:

- *The most passionate person I know is...*

- *My Passion has resulted in...*

- *The three most positive observations my closest friends would make about my Superpower Passion are...*

Superpower PASSION

Your Superpower illuminates like a spotlight when the object of your Passion takes center stage in your life.

Regardless of whether it's an idea, principle, creation or person, your illuminating spotlight makes it easy for others to see, become inspired by and share your Passion.

NOTE TO SELF:

PASSION

is just one of my many Superpowers

CHAPTER 32

PATIENCE: Defined

- *steadfast despite adversity or length of process*

PATIENCE: in Action

Complete the following sentences:

- *The person I know with the most Patience is...*

- *Their Patience has...*

- *The most powerful results of my Patience have been...*

- *The three most positive observations my closest friends would make about my Superpower Patience are...*

Superpower PATIENCE

Your Superpower Patience is likely more visible to those around you at first than it is to you. When it becomes a way of life for you, it's difficult for you to see that this profound gift is one of your most precious Superpowers.

Like a farmer who has planted a seed in the ground confident it will germinate, even though for a good amount of time there is no evidence of growth, your Patience is steadfast when there is no visible sign your vision is coming to life. Just as the farmer's seed grows up pushing through the heavy soil, your Patience allows you to push past resistance and obstacles in your path.

With Patience as your Superpower, you never lose sight of what you have set out to accomplish no matter how long or strenuous the process.

NOTE TO SELF:

PATIENCE

is just one of my many Superpowers

CHAPTER 33

PEACEMAKER: Defined

- *person who reconciles parties who disagree*

PEACEMAKER: in Action

Complete the following sentences:

- *My favorite Peacemaker is...*

- *They result of their actions were...*

- *I was considered a Peacemaker when...*

- *The three most positive observations my closest friends would make about my Superpower Peacemaker are...*

Superpower PEACEMAKER

Your Superpower Peacemaker ensures you create an environment of understanding, empathy and win-win compromise. Those in your circle of influence are in awe of your abilities to move projects forward and achieve amazing results even with teams of people who have vastly different ideas and opinions. Respecting all differences, you inspire others to look for ways to set egos aside to incorporate and support the best ideas even if they are not their own.

If everyone in the world activated this Superpower at the same time, we would achieve world peace.

NOTE TO SELF:

PEACEMAKER

is just one of my many Superpowers

CHAPTER 34

PERSISTENCE: Defined

-   *to go on resolutely in spite of opposition or warning*

PERSISTENCE: in Action

Complete the following sentences:

- *The most persistent person I know is...*

- *Because of their Persistence...*

- *Persistence is how I accomplished...*

- *The three most positive observations my closest friends would make about my Superpower Persistence are...*

Superpower PERSISTENCE

Your Persistence is the Superpower that keeps
you moving forward and overcoming obstacles in
your path. Like a plow cultivating rocky, hardened
earth, your Persistence eventually softens or
moves even your most resistant opponents.

This Superpower draws on your other Superpowers of
Creativity and Persuasion to help you find new ways
to succeed at whatever you decide to accomplish.

NOTE TO SELF:

PERSISTENCE

is just one of my many Superpowers

CHAPTER 35

PERSUASION: Defined

-   *the act of moving another to a belief, position or course of action*

PERSUASION: in Action

Complete the following sentences:

- *The most persuasive person I know is...*

- *I was most persuasive when...*

- *My acts of persuasion resulted in...*

- *The three most positive observations my closest friends would make about my Superpower Persuasion are...*

Superpower PERSUASION

Your Superpower Persuasion creates a magnetic force that draws others into your beliefs and actions. Persuading others to believe as you do comes so naturally at times that you don't even recognize this Superpower within yourself.

Those with this Superpower often choose careers in teaching, sales or politics. The strength of this Superpower within you is in direct relation to the strength of your beliefs. Your Persuasion creates a chain reaction activating those around you who activate those around them.

Activating this Superpower for good also may involve activating your Humility and Integrity Superpowers.

NOTE TO SELF:

PERSUASION

is just one of my many Superpowers

CHAPTER 36

PLAYFUL: Defined

- *taking part in fun recreation*

PLAYFUL: In Action

Complete the following sentences:

- *The most Playful adult I know is…*

- *They inspire me to be more Playful when…*

- *I am most Playful when…*

- *The three most positive observations my closest friends would make about my Superpower Playful are…*

Superpower PLAYFUL

When your Playful Superpower is activated, it's almost like you're the Pied Piper, everyone wants to follow along. Sometimes, your playfulness is revealed through conversation or mentally stimulating games and sometimes it flourishes with recreational physical activity. It is very much like you to be the childlike adult in the group that's daring everyone to try something new.

Being Playful keeps you and those around you full of life and always young at heart.

NOTE TO SELF:

PLAYFUL

is just one of my many Superpowers

CHAPTER 37

PRAYER: Defined

- *a devout petition to God*

PRAYER: in Action

Complete the following sentences:

- *I learned to pray when...*

- *When I pray...*

- *My prayers have resulted in...*

- *The three most positive observations my closest friends would make about my Superpower Prayer are...*

Superpower **PRAYER**

Prayer is the most powerful of all your Superpowers. It is activated the moment you are consciously engaged with your higher power. Whether silent or audible, this Superpower is constantly available for activation. When engaged in Prayer, your Superpower is drawing positive energy from the universe, creating a synergy around the focus of your Prayer.

Answers to your prayers are not always clear. However, the positive effects are unlimited.

NOTE TO SELF:

PRAYER

is just one of my many Superpowers

CHAPTER 38

SERENITY: Defined

- *Calm, confident peace within*

SERENITY: in Action

Complete the following sentences:

- *The person who brings Serenity to life is...*

- *When I experienced Serenity, I was...*

- *The three most positive observations my closest friends would make about my Superpower Serenity are...*

Superpower SERENITY

This Superpower is most appreciated when it is lost and then found. This is the most important Superpower for your overall health and well-being. It must be activated regularly for your gifts to be effectively shared with others.

Activation of this Superpower is very personal and may be inspired by music or sounds like birds chirping or waves crashing. It could be triggered by seeing or imagining beautiful scenes like rolling hills, a field of flowers or a sunset over the ocean. Serenity also could be activated by smells or tastes like the smell and taste of a steaming cup of hot chocolate.

The greatest benefit of this Superpower is that it gives you the ability to calmly and peacefully accept the things you cannot change.

When you are fully in the moment with no concern about the past or future, you have activated Serenity. Enjoy this Superpower for yourself many times each day and others will find theirs in you.

NOTE TO SELF:

SERENITY

is just one of my many Superpowers

CHAPTER 39

SISTER: Defined

-    *having a close relationship with another because of shared interests or concerns*

SISTER: In Action

Complete the following sentences:

- *The people in my life whom I consider Sisters are...*

- *The experiences we shared that bonded us as Sisters include...*

- *I am most proud of the moments I was a Sister when...*

- *The three most positive observations my closest friends would make about my Superpower Sister are...*

Superpower SISTER

There are many people who have enjoyed and continue to benefit from connecting with you as a Sister. This innate Superpower is a bond that goes beyond gender or family relations. This incredible Superpower is like an emotional glue that keeps you connected as a Sister, even when facing the most challenging issues.

Those who call you Sister know they can count on you for the best type of support at the exact time it is most needed.

NOTE TO SELF:

SISTER

is just one of my many Superpowers

CHAPTER 40

SPIRIT: Defined

- *the activating or essential principle influencing action*

SPIRIT: In Action

Complete the following sentences:

- *The person I know with the most Spirit is...*

- *Their actions resulted in...*

- *My Spirit soars when...*

- *The three most positive observations my closest friends would make about my Superpower Spirit are...*

Superpower SPIRIT

Your Superpower Spirit is generated from within and is always with you. Regardless of your circumstances in life, your Spirit is your true-life force that is never seen but always felt by those around you.

As an invisible force field around you, it either draws others to you in support of a passion or gently keeps others at a distance to allow your Spirit to heal and regenerate when needed.

Your Spirit Superpower will activate on its own by igniting other Superpowers when needed to see you through even the most prolonged or threatening situations in your life.

NOTE TO SELF:

SPIRIT

is just one of my many Superpowers

CHAPTER 41

STABILIZER: Defined

- *to hold steady*

STABILIZER: In Action

Complete the following sentences:

- *Complete the following sentences...*

- *The most Stable person I know is...*

- *As they Stabilize a situation, people around them...*

- *When I am most Stable I...*

- *The three most positive observations my closest friends would make about my Superpower Stabilizer are...*

Superpower STABILIZER

When those around you are gyrating out of control, your Superpower activates, and you inspire a calm, stable environment. You become the voice of reason. Like the solid foundation of a house, your Superpower is often taken for granted. At times, your Superpower is misunderstood by those that want to sweep you into their chaos.

Remain the steadfast voice of reason, the world could use more Stabilizers like you.

NOTE TO SELF:

STABILIZER

is just one of my many Superpowers

CHAPTER 42

STAMINA: Defined

- *the power to endure*

STAMINA: In Action

Complete the following sentences:

- *The person I know who has shown the most Stamina is...*

- *Their Stamina has...*

- *I have shown Stamina when...*

- *The three most positive observations my closest friends would make about my Superpower Stamina are...*

Superpower STAMINA

Like a string tethered to your chest gently pulling you up and forward, your Superpower Stamina ensures you endure even the most difficult obstacles. Every long-distance runner employs this Superpower to finish the race, enduring their own aches and pains as well as course obstacles. Stamina is the Superpower that sees you through raising children, building a company, battling an illness or healing nations rife with conflict.

Your Stamina inspires others in ways you may never know. Your ability to share how this incredible Superpower affects your life adds even greater influence and inspires others to activate their own Superpower Stamina.

NOTE TO SELF:

STAMINA

is just one of my many Superpowers

CHAPTER 43

STRATEGIC: Defined

-    *one who employs a series of maneuvers for obtaining a goal*

STRATEGIC: In Action

Complete the following sentences:

- *The most Strategic person I know is…*

- *The series of maneuvers they made to achieve their goal were…*

- *As a Strategic I have reached an important goal by…*

- *The three most positive observations my closest friends would make about my Superpower Strategic are…*

Superpower STRATEGIC

Your Strategic Superpower is at its peak when you have activated your Visionary, Logic, Intuition, Persistence and Patience Superpowers. Visionary helps you clearly see your goal and all the benefits of achieving that goal. Logic ensures you map out all the steps and maneuvers needed to reach that goal. Intuition gives you the ability to adjust the steps as needed to overcome obstacles. Persistence keeps you moving forward on your path regardless of the resistance that is sure to present itself. Patience keeps you on the path no matter how much time it takes or resistance you encounter.

Your Strategic Superpower is the super conductor that directs the symphony of all the other Superpowers activated toward your desired outcome.

NOTE TO SELF:

STRATEGIC

is just one of my many Superpowers

CHAPTER 44

TEACHER: Defined

- *a person who imparts knowledge*

TEACHER: In Action

Complete the following sentences:

- *The best Teacher I know is...*

- *I have been most inspired by their ability to Teach when...*

- *I have been a Teacher when...*

- *My ability to Teach has...*

- *The three most positive observations my closest friends would make about my Superpower Teacher are...*

Superpower TEACHER

What makes your Superpower Teacher so unique is that everyone you touch is eager to learn from you. It may be months, years or even decades before you fully realize the impact you have made on someone's life.

This Superpower is activated consciously and unconsciously, whether you are passing along specific instructions or are a living example.

In some cases, you are not even aware your Teacher Superpower had a positive effect until one of your protégés has activated their own Teacher Superpower that was kindled by your passion.

As a Teacher you are perpetually inspiring future Teachers.

Thank you.

NOTE TO SELF:

TEACHER

is just one of my many Superpowers

CHAPTER 45

TOLERANCE: Defined

- *a fair, objective, permissive attitude toward those whose opinions or beliefs are different than your own*

TOLERANCE: In Action

Complete the following sentence:

- *The person I know with the most Tolerance is...*

- *Their Tolerance has...*

- *My Tolerance has...*

- *The three most positive observations my closest friends would make about my Superpower Tolerance are...*

Superpower TOLERANCE

Your Superpower Tolerance has an incredible worldwide impact even though you may never see or experience the ripple effect of your actions and attitudes.

The need for Tolerance is universal. The world is filled with billions of unique individuals who are exposed to smaller societies. Within each society there are expectations of conformity to specific beliefs and in many a disdain for or fear of differences.

Your Superpower cuts through the ingrained beliefs and attitudes of intolerant generations to create an environment of acceptance, mutual respect and even more people activating their own Superpower Tolerance.

NOTE TO SELF:

TOLERANCE

is just one of my many Superpowers

CHAPTER 46

TRANQUILITY: Defined

- *a calm, peaceful, gentle quietness that permeates and regenerates your body and soul*

TRANQUILITY: In Action

Complete the following sentences:

- *The most Tranquil person I know is...*

- *The places I find Tranquility are...*

- *I am most Tranquil when...*

- *The three most positive observations my closest friends would make about my Superpower Tranquility are...*

Superpower TRANQUILITY

When you finally activate your Superpower Tranquility, it's as if the whole world has become still, quiet and peaceful.

When you first realized the magnitude of this incredible Superpower, you may have experienced a great deal of turmoil in your life. However, once activated, your Superpower Tranquility can always be accessed again on conscience command, no matter how much turmoil is going on around you.

Tranquility allows you to be confident that your life is on course and no matter what lies ahead you are ready.

Those in your presence sense your Tranquility and are more likely to find it within themselves as well, perpetuating the wonder of this Superpower.

NOTE TO SELF:

TRANQUILITY

is just one of my many Superpowers

CHAPTER 47

TRANSFORMER: Defined

- *person who changes the composition, structure, appearance or character of a situation*

TRANSFORMER: in Action

Complete the following sentences:

- *The person I know that has transformed something tragic into something great is...*

- *I have had the opportunity to transform...*

- *My actions resulted in...*

- *The three most positive observations my closest friends would make about my Superpower Transformer are...*

Superpower TRANSFORMER

Your Superpower gives you the ability to transform any situation, no matter how bad, into something good and profound. You know that to access your Superpower first requires an internal shift from seeing the situation as bad into seeing the situation as an opportunity. Your Transformer Superpowers then create a chain reaction of positive events around you.

Sometimes the process is slow and methodical with many small changes taking effect. However, there are times as a Transformer when you move the process along quickly with sweeping obvious conversions.

Imagine a world where everyone activates this Superpower to transform poverty to wealth for all.

NOTE TO SELF:

TRANSFORMER

is just one of my many Superpowers

CHAPTER 48

VALOR: Defined

- *boldness or determination in facing great danger*

VALOR: IN ACTION

Complete the following sentences:

- *The person I know who shows the most Valor is...*

- *Their Valor helped...*

- *An example of when my own Valor was put to the test was when...*

- *The three most positive observations my closest friends would make about my Superpower Valor are...*

Superpower VALOR

When you or your loved ones are faced with grave danger, your Superpowers of Bravery, Courage and Warrior are activated. When they are all activated at the same time, a fourth Superpower emerges - Valor.

This is the Superpower that propels you forward through the most difficult life-threatening events in your life. You have most likely experienced activating these Superpowers in service to others - often without them even knowing it.

Thank you!

NOTE TO SELF:

VALOR

is just one of my many Superpowers

CHAPTER 49

VISIONARY: Defined

- *a person with unusually clear foresight*

VISIONARY: In Action

Complete the following sentences:

- *The most Visionary person I know is...*

- *As a Visionary they have...*

- *As a Visionary I have...*

- *The three most positive observations my closest friends would make about my Superpower Visionary are...*

Superpower VISIONARY

Your Visionary Superpower seems to others like you have your own crystal ball that gives you a glimpse into the future.

In reality, your Visionary Superpower is not mystical, but is a result of understanding the steps needed to fulfill your vision or dream. It keeps you on your path even when obstacles require you to take detours.

No matter how long or arduous the journey, you never lose sight of your vision along the way.

Although activated during the entire journey, arriving at your destination and realizing success is when your Visionary Superpower is most often recognized and celebrated.

NOTE TO SELF:

VISIONARY

is just one of my many Superpowers

CHAPTER 50

WARRIOR: Defined

- *a person engaged in overcoming destructive conflict*

WARRIOR: IN ACTION

Complete the following sentences:

- *The fiercest Warrior I know is…*

- *Their Warrior actions resulted in…*

- *As a Warrior, I…*

- *The results of my Warrior actions were…*

- *The three most positive observations my closest friends would make about my Superpower Warrior are…*

Superpower WARRIOR

The Warrior Superpower in you is activated instinctively when you or those around you need protection. Although assertive action is often all that is required, you are willing to take the necessary steps of aggression to protect those in your care.

Your Warrior Superpower is used primarily in service to others. Personally knowing the individuals you are protecting isn't required for your Warrior instincts to move you to action.

You are often considered a hero by those that know you and the actions you've taken. However, simply knowing your actions have resulted in protecting those you serve is your greatest reward.

NOTE TO SELF:

WARRIOR

is just one of my many Superpowers

CHAPTER 51

WISDOM: Defined

- *accumulated learning*

WISDOM: in Action

Complete the following sentences:

- *The person I know who displays the most profound Wisdom is...*

- *I have shown Wisdom by...*

- *The three most positive observations my closest friends would make about my Superpower Wisdom are...*

Superpower WISDOM

Wisdom is the most often coveted Superpower you have. Yes, you have wisdom as a Superpower even though you have sought and likely will continue to seek this precious gift the rest of your life.

Activating this Superpower happens in stages -- over time. Think of a toddler learning to walk for the first time. They are wobbly, and every step is a conscious action. Then walking becomes a habit and the unconscious memory of how to walk takes over. The toddler is now ready to learn how to run or climb.

Wisdom is activated this same way. First, you are conscious and maybe even self-conscious of your new knowledge. Then, that knowledge is stored in your unconscious, leaving your conscious to gain new knowledge and access previously stored information as needed.

Wisdom is your Superpower that is most unique to you. The pace at which it grows is always your decision.

NOTE TO SELF:

WISDOM

is just one of my many Superpowers

CHAPTER 52

WOMAN: Defined

- *distinctively feminine nature*

WOMAN: IN ACTION

Complete the following sentences:

- *The most powerful Woman I know is…*

- *Her actions resulted in…*

- *I have felt the most feminine and powerful when…*

- *The three most positive observations my closest friends would make about my Superpower Woman are…*

Superpower WOMAN

Regardless of your gender or age this Superpower can begin developing at any stage of your life. When exerting your independence to be free from restrictions, control or dictatorial influence is critical for survival or growth your Superpower Woman emerges and activates other Superpowers to improve your situation.

Whether the circumstances call for assertive action or gentle understanding, as this Superpower develops within you, you'll know how to be and inspire others to be the best Woman for good.

NOTE TO SELF:

WOMAN

is just one of my many Superpowers

WEEKLY JOURNAL

Record your hopes, dreams, desires, stories,
observations, and personal achievements
for an inspiring, Super-empowered life.

WEEK 1 Dream big.

WEEK 2 You're worth it!

WEEK 3 Refresh your soul

WEEK 4 Plan a retreat

WEEK 5 Tell a friend their Superpower you admire

WEEK 6 Explore a new hobby

WEEK 7 Live it up

WEEK 8 Laugh out loud

WEEK 9 Take a nap

WEEK 10 Snuggle with a loved one

WEEK 11 Dance

WEEK 12 Sing

WEEK 13 Surrender to this moment

WEEK 14 Find purpose

WEEK 15 Cry out loud

WEEK 16 Look for a rainbow

WEEK 17 Count a blessing

WEEK 18 Fall up

WEEK 19 Soar

WEEK 20 Open your eyes

WEEK 21 Go for a walk

WEEK 22 Say hi to your neighbor

WEEK 23 Schedule your annual health check-up

WEEK 24 Plan a retreat

WEEK 25 Call an old friend

WEEK 26 Learn something new

WEEK 27 Plan a family meal

WEEK 28 Tell a joke

WEEK 29 Congratulate someone

WEEK 30 Say a silent prayer for someone

WEEK 31 Close your eyes

WEEK 32 Savor the moment

WEEK 33 Celebrate your accomplishments

WEEK 34 Volunteer your time for something you Love

WEEK 35 Invite a friend to lunch

WEEK 36 Leave your watch at home

WEEK 37 Turn off your phone for 20 minutes

WEEK 38 Meditate

WEEK 39 Bless your mother

WEEK 40 Bless your father

WEEK 41 Close your eye

WEEK 42 Imagine you are surrounded by love and light

WEEK 43 Declare a personal Holiday

WEEK 44 Plan a trip

WEEK 45 Learn something new

WEEK 46 Share your knowledge

WEEK 47 Walk a new path

WEEK 48 Watch a sunset

WEEK 49 Wear comfortable shoes

WEEK 50 Read a good book

WEEK 51 Look for Joy

WEEK 52 Celebrate your style

BONUS WEEK Congratulate yourself and start again

THE YEAR AHEAD

IN CONCLUSION

Superpowers Activated was originally designed for a full year, 52-weeks of contemplating a different Superpower. However, the original Superpower list contained more than 70 words.

Although some turned out to be very similar to the words chosen, it still seemed impossible to cut out so many Superpowers. As you have probably discovered on your own by now, you have even more Superpowers than are described here.

The Bonus Chapter helped me include one more for you.

I chose Winner because I believe anyone who takes even a little amount of time recognizing the good in others and devotes energy to develop their own strengths is a Winner.

If you'd like to stay connected, subscribe to our weekly e-newsletter at Superpowers365.com/Connect.

Let's soar,

Debbie Donaldson
Champion for Good

p.s. If you loved the book, please give us a review on Amazon.com.

BONUS CHAPTER

WINNER: Defined

- one who is successful, especially through ability or hard work

WINNER: in Action

Complete the following sentences:

- *The people I consider WINNERS are...*

- *I have been a WINNER at...*

- *The three most positive observations my closest friends would make about my Superpower Winner are...*

Superpower WINNER

This Superpower within you can hardly be contained by your physical body. At times being a Winner seems as exciting as sparkling water in your veins. At other times as a Winner, you are so calm you feel weightless, as if you are floating in air. Either way, those around you are caught up in your emotions.

You take the responsibility of this Superpower seriously. As a Winner you find ways to share and celebrate this Superpower, making those around you crave more time in your presence. Your example provides others the opportunity to recognize and develop their own Superpowers to become Winners.

NOTE TO SELF:

WINNER

is just one of my many Superpowers

Tell a friend their Superpowers you admire.

"The magic of Superpowers is discovered by experiencing them in the actions of those around us; in recognizing them through our own actions; and in how we believe others perceive them in the way we live."

Debbie Donaldson

www.ingramcontent.com/pod-product-compliance
Lightning Source LLC
LaVergne TN
LVHW051541080426
835510LV00020B/2808